Tunnels, Nitro and Convicts

Building the Railroad That Couldn't Be Built

By Stephen R. Little
Marion, North Carolina

AuthorHouse™
1663 Liberty Drive
Bloomington, IN 47403
www.authorhouse.com
Phone: 833-262-8899

Because of the dynamic nature of the Internet, any web addresses or links contained in this book may have changed
since publication and may no longer be valid. The views expressed in this work are solely those of the author and do not
necessarily reflect the views of the publisher, and the publisher hereby disclaims any responsibility for them.

Any people depicted in stock imagery provided by Getty Images are models,
and such images are being used for illustrative purposes only.
Certain stock imagery © Getty Images.

This book is printed on acid-free paper.

ISBN: 978-1-4520-6771-1 (sc)

Print information available on the last page.

Published by AuthorHouse 10/30/2021

authorHOUSE®

Tunnels, Nitro and Convicts is dedicated to the wonderful memory of the late Warren E. Hobbs, the author's much loved brother-in-law and friend, who inspired and encouraged people of all ages and conditions.

Lick Log Tunnel. Photo by Rufus Morgan c. 1877. North Carolina
Collection. Univ. of N.C. Library at Chapel Hill.

Tunnels, Nitro and Convicts
Building the Railroad That Couldn't Be Built

"Grandpa," asked Andy in the year 1874, "why does the railroad end at Henry Station? Why doesn't it go up the mountain and on to Asheville?" "There's a mighty good reason," Grandpa answered. "It can't be done. The mountain is too steep. People will just have to keep riding the stage coach up to Ridgecrest and on to Asheville."

He was referring to the tall mountain in the western edge of McDowell County, North Carolina. At the top of the mountain is the Eastern Continental Divide. Rain falling on the west side of the mountain eventually flows into the Gulf of Mexico. Rain falling on the east side ends up in the Atlantic Ocean.

Andy's Grandpa wasn't wrong very often. But this time he was wrong. Starting in 1875, the largest earth-moving project ever seen in the United States took place between Old Fort and Ridgecrest. The project? Building the railroad up and over the mountain. The one that people thought couldn't be built.

To understand what it was like when Andy talked with his Grandpa in 1875, you have to close your eyes and use your imagination. Imagine the world's largest dump truck, overflowing with dirt, huge boulders, bushes and trees. It is slowly backing up on Interstate 40, inching its way east from Asheville, North Carolina. As it reaches the Eastern Continental Divide at the top of the mountain at Ridgecrest, it slows to a stop.

The dumper on the world's largest dump truck then starts to rise, and all the dirt and boulders and bushes and trees start to slide out and completely fill up the 6-lane highway. It covers up the road, all the way down the mountain to Old Fort. When the dust settles, there is not a highway any more ...just a thick, beautiful forest.

That's what it was like in 1875. That's what it was like when the Revolutionary War was being fought a hundred years earlier, and that's what it was like when Davidson's Fort provided a place of safety at Old Fort for the earliest local settlers when there was conflict between the settlers and the native Indians.

Too Steep to Build the Railroad?

Andy knew the Indians had figured out hundreds of years ago the best way to walk up and over the mountain. Grandpa told him that pioneer settlers used part of the Indian path to make a narrow dirt road barely wide enough for buckboard wagons and a small stagecoach to make the bumpy trip.

Andy's Grandpa explained that trains have to travel on a flat smooth track that has to be laid on a straight, even grade. Trains can't make sharp turns and they can't go up (or safely go down!) steep hills. That means low areas have to be built up and high areas have to be trimmed down or have tunnels constructed. Maybe some bridges or trestles have to be built across ravines or streams.

Railroads were already one of the main ways people and their crops and belongings traveled long distances all over the rest of North Carolina and the United States. The famous golden spike had been hammered to link the country's eastern and western railroad networks in 1869. When the civil war ended in 1865, droves of adventure-seeking soldiers went west to speed up its construction.

The State of North Carolina Conducts a Railroad-Building Experiment

Since long before the Civil War, North Carolina's leaders wanted to build the railroad all the way across the state ... from the Atlantic coast on the east to the Tennessee border in the west. By 1875, six years after the transcontinental railroad connection, the railroad in North Carolina ran from the east coast only as far as Henry Station, just west of Old Fort. That's where it stopped, at the base of the daunting steepness of the eastern continental divide.

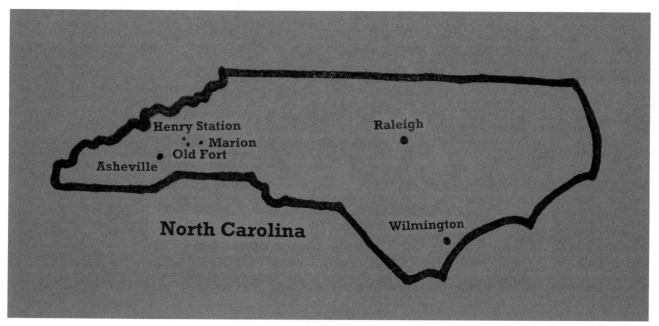

North Carolina.

In 1855, the state created a company called the Western North Carolina Railroad, and started working on a plan to build the railroad that couldn't be built! Walter Gwynn was a design engineer who trampled through the mountains and identified the route that was chosen in 1859.

The **Mountain Division** of the Western North Carolina Railroad started at Henry Station and went uphill to the western side of the Swannanoa Mountain.

Even though the straight-line distance of the Mountain Division was only 3.4 miles ("as the crow flies," Andy's Grandpa called it), the steep grade of the mountains presented the greatest challenge that railroad builders had ever faced as they tried to make their way across North Carolina.

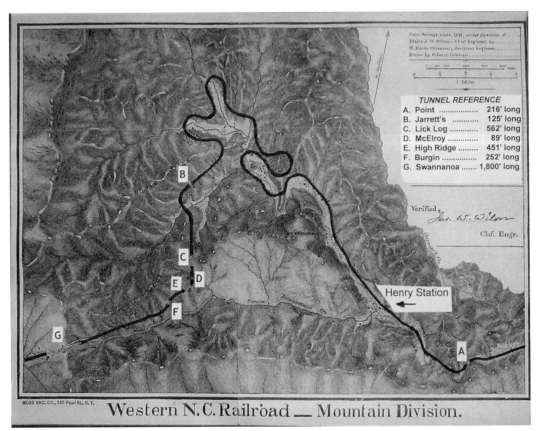

TUNNEL REFERENCE
A. Point .... 216' long
B. Jarrett's .... 125' long
C. Lick Log .... 562' long
D. McElroy .... 89' long
E. High Ridge .... 451' long
F. Burgin .... 252' long
G. Swannanoa .... 1,800' long

Western N.C. Railroad — Mountain Division.

- Major James W. Wilson's 1881 survey of the Mountain Division.

The State of North Carolina did not have enough money in 1875 to pay for all the tools, equipment, supplies and labor that would be needed for this huge Mountain Division railroad construction project. The civil war had ended only 10 years earlier, and there were still many expensive projects that needed to be done, but there was not much money. The state's leaders determined that the time was right to begin work, so the railroad builders had to create ways to do their job without using much money from the public treasury.

People in eastern North Carolina wanted to help with the railroad. It would allow the folks in the mountains to buy products raised or made down east and other items imported through the ports in eastern NC. People in the coastal city of Wilmington, the largest North Carolina port on the Atlantic Ocean, raised money to buy tools and rails for this ambitious project that was hundreds of miles away from them.

- The people of coastal Wilmington, N.C. raised money to buy iron rails.

A state-wide railroad would also allow the mountaineers to send their crops and products across the state to customers and ports at the Atlantic coast. Without a railroad connecting the mountains and coast of North Carolina, it was easier and closer for the mountain people to travel through the valleys to the South Carolina coastal ports to buy and sell products.

Henry Station and Round Knob

Henry Station was the name of the end-of-the-line spot for the railroad just west of Old Fort. A small wooden structure was there that contained a railroad office and supervisor's headquarters. Henry Station became the center of operations for the Mountain Division railroad construction project. (Henry Station was located in the field that today can be seen between the railroad tracks and Mill Creek Road, across from the entrance to the National Park Service Picnic Area on Old US Highway 70 just west of Old Fort.)

- Henry Station, c. 1876. North Carolina Collection at Pack
Memorial Public Library, Asheville, N.C.

A small, private hotel was built about the time work on the Mountain Division was underway, at a pretty spot called Round Knob about two miles northwest of Henry Station. Until the railroad was completed, many passengers stayed overnight at Round Knob Lodge while waiting for the small overland stagecoach. It made only one trip per day on a rough and uncomfortable trail from Round Knob to the area now known as Ridgecrest at the top of the steep Swannanoa Mountain.

Free Labor from Prison Convicts

Now that the State of North Carolina was in the railroad-building business, one of the biggest problems was getting people to do the hard construction work and figuring out how to pay them. To solve this issue, the State took advantage of a large supply of free labor: prison convicts. The convicts had just completed the major construction project of building Central Prison in Raleigh (which housed convicted felons for almost one hundred years), and the state warden declared they needed to do something worthwhile.

With authorization by the North Carolina Legislature, convicts from the North Carolina state prison were brought over from Raleigh to do most of the work on the railroad-building project. The first 35 convicts arrived at Henry Station in late October of 1875. Over the next seven months, 265 more men and 16 women inmates arrived to work on this amazing construction project. One year later, convicts had performed a total of 80,309 days of work! More and more convicts continued to be shipped from Raleigh to work on this huge project.

The convicts' first job was to cut enough trees to clear the sites and build bunkhouse-type stockades as places for them to sleep at night. Bunkhouse stockades were eventually built in five locations along the project route. The first one was about two miles west of Henry Station and was called the Round Knob Stockade. Lick Log Stockade was next, located near Lick Log tunnel. A third stockade was built at the top of the mountain, near the Swannanoa tunnel, and it was called the Swannanoa Stockade or the Top of the Mountain Stockade.

Two more, the Long Branch Stockade and the Tomahawk Stockade, were built in the middle area of the Mountain Division. Each stockade was large enough to have crude bunks for 125 convicts. The stockades were quite hot in the summer and were extremely cold in the winter.

After completing the stockades, the convicts quickly started to work under the direction of Major James W. Wilson, the project's Chief Engineer. They began clearing a very smooth path for the rails. When shorter hills were in the way where the rails needed to be laid, the convicts dug out open areas called "open cuts" so that the rails could stay on an even grade. Sometimes they had to build strong trestles to support the rails that needed to cross over ravines and streams.

- Wooden trestles crossing a ravine near Round Knob. 1972.

When there were taller hills and ridges in the way, they had to dig tunnels! Another daily assignment for one group of convicts was cutting trees to supply firewood and timber for making cross-ties to support the rails. The women inmates did the cooking, clothes mending and washing, and the injured and the older convicts made soap, buckets and candles.

The convicts' living and working conditions were severe and extremely dangerous. No matter how hot it got in the summer, and no matter how cold it got in the winter, they worked almost every day. Only winter's worst ice storms and deepest snows stopped the work on the Mountain Division. A routine 6 to 8 inch snowfall was not enough reason to stop the work. An accumulation of over two feet of snow was once documented as a valid reason for work being suspended temporarily.

Some local men who had grown up in the mountains were hired to provide very valuable knowledge about the mountain geography, weather and culture. These local men helped persuade the mountain people that the large group of convicts working on the railroad should be left alone so they could work. Some of the local men were supervisors and overseers of the huge project.

Local men near Burgin Tunnel, including John Lytle Stepp (left), a foreman, great grandfather of Becky Garrou of Old Fort, NC.

Six Tunnels in Less than Three Miles

Six tunnels were dug out by convicts in the Mountain Division, plus one more (known as Point Tunnel) between Old Fort and Henry Station. All six in the Mountain Division are in the western-most 2.5 miles. From east to west, these tunnels are: Jarrett's, Lick Log, McElroy, High Ridge, Burgin and Swannanoa Tunnel. The shortest was McElroy Tunnel at 89 feet and the longest was the Swannanoa Tunnel at the crest of the eastern continental divide, extending 1800 feet through the heart of Swannanoa Mountain.

The next-to-longest was Lick Log Tunnel, which was 562 feet long ... almost as long as two football fields! Each tunnel had to be 15 feet tall to provide adequate clearance for the tall smokestacks on the old wood-burning locomotives.

Jarrett's Tunnel, looking east, 1972.

– Jarrett's Tunnel, looking west. 2010.

Fifteen feet doesn't sound very tall until you try to find something that is 15 feet tall! If Andy had stood on Grandpa's shoulders, he still could not have reached the ceiling of the tunnels. Doors in most houses are not quite 7 feet tall. The tunnels were taller than two doors stacked on top of each other! But for the top of the tunnel to be 15 feet above the rails, the ground had to be dug out more than 15 feet from the top. Enough of the rough, uneven rock had to be broken up and removed so that dirt could be brought in and packed down to create a smooth surface. Then the crossties and rails were added. That's when the fifteen feet distance was measured.

Burgin Tunnel's rock walls and ceiling. 2010.

- Rock walls and ceiling of Jarrett's Tunnel. 2010.

Hammering through the earth into part of a mountain required more muscle and hard work than you can imagine. Sometimes the convicts were digging out dirt, but most of the time it was a mass of hard, solid rock that had to be removed. It became dark about 15 feet into the mountain. Looking back toward the opening created a glare that made it difficult to see where the hammer needed to hit. With their backs to the opening, the light grew more dim with each step deeper into the rock. After all, until the tunnel is opened on both ends, it is just a long, deep, dark cave.

- Western portal of High Ridge Tunnel. 1972.

There is another problem when digging a tunnel. There are lots of small springs in the mountains, and water would often drip into the tunnels. That made it very slippery and therefore very dangerous to be pounding and slamming a heavy sledge hammer in the wet, dark tunnel. Also, the convicts would get wet from the seeping, dripping water and did not have a good way to get dry. Being wet while exposed to cold winter weather was very dangerous.

As the chief designer and engineer of the railroad project, Major Wilson had the huge task of making sure that the tracks would continue to climb as they moved west. Just as the sloping grade had to keep moving up outside the tunnels, it also had to keep climbing inside the tunnels.

High Ridge Tunnel posed yet another staggering problem. That tunnel curves as it goes through the solid rock! As the locomotive enters one end, the conductor cannot see the other end. The other opening (called a portal) is not visible until after the train turns along the curve inside the tunnel.

- Dark, curving rock wall and ceiling inside High Ridge Tunnel. 2010.

The most time-consuming work involved in excavating a tunnel was hauling out the heavy broken rock from its walls and ceiling. Convicts would have to load it all into large wooden carts and wheelbarrows. They would then push the heavy, full carts and wheelbarrows out of the cave (it was not yet a tunnel!).

Once they got the carts out, they had to keep on pushing so they could dump the heavy rock and dirt to fill in low areas on the track route. Filling in and building up some of the ravines and low areas was just as much hard work as removing the dirt and rock for the open cuts and tunnels. The work was brutally hard. A report to the NC Legislature in February 1879 mentioned "eight or ten convicts pulling and pushing a cart, [doing] the work of one mule...."

- Looking east through Burgin Tunnel. 1972.

The excavation of the tunnels involved digging with pick and shovel as far as possible. Sometimes the convicts had to use gun powder ("black powder") to break up the solid rock with blasting explosions. Black powder was expensive, however, and mostly the convicts had to keep hitting and hammering away at the rocks to break them up.

- Very little room to spare between the rails and rock walls inside Burgin Tunnel. 2010.

Other than daylight coming in from the opening, the only light in the tunnels was provided by candles made by other convicts. Pounding a heavy hammer in a dark, wet tunnel is as hard as it is dangerous ... both for the convict working with the sledge hammer and for others around him picking up pieces of broken rock.

Pushing a Locomotive through the Dirt up a Mountain

In the summer of 1877, in an attempt to speed up completion of the Swannanoa Tunnel, Major Wilson ordered the only wood-burning locomotive on the Mountain Division to be moved from Henry Station to the western portal of the Swannanoa Tunnel. The locomotive, known as the _Salisbury_, and its tender car (which holds the wood for fuel and water to be heated by burning the wood, to produce steam) had to be pushed up the mountain, overland to the crest of the ridge on the western side of the Eastern Continental Divide.

The convicts gathered around both sides of the locomotive as it sat on the tracks. Using all their strength, they picked up the _Salisbury_ off the tracks, walked it over several feet, and put it down on temporary rails spiked directly to the ground! Then, with help from several oxen and mules, they pushed and pulled the incredibly heavy locomotive several miles up the mountain along the stage road between Henry Station and Ridgecrest ... all the way to the top of the mountain!

- The _Salisbury_, pulling passengers and freight near Old Fort, c. 1885, after the Mountain Division was finished.

As the locomotive was dragged and pulled and pushed along the temporary track, the convicts picked up the rails from the ground just covered and re-laid them in front, always making sure they stayed at the same width. Because the locomotive was so heavy, the convicts could not ever stop pushing and pulling until they got to the top, as the _Salisbury_ would have rolled backwards off the rails.

If the _Salisbury_ had rolled off the rails, it could have gotten stuck in the dirt. The convicts would have had to pick it up again to put it back on the tracks. Even worse, it could have fallen on its side.

Just as hard as pushing and pulling the locomotive up the mountain was the job of holding it back as they crested the top and began to go downhill to the western portal of the Swannanoa Tunnel. They could not relax even for a minute until the job was completed and the _Salisbury_ was on the tracks outside the tunnel.

The convicts did not use crossties under most of the temporary rails, but they still had to keep the path smooth and flat. The weight of the _Salisbury_ would have bent the rails if the ground under them had not been smooth and level. To cross streams, low areas or muddy spots, rocks and logs had to be put under the rails to make the path as smooth and level as possible.

Can you imagine the total amazement of passengers in the daily stagecoach as they saw a locomotive in the middle of the woods surrounded by a group of striped-shirted convicts pushing and pulling it along the stage road!

When the locomotive finally arrived at the western portal of the Swannanoa Tunnel, the convicts had to pick it up again and put it down on the real tracks. After the locomotive was in place, the convicts repeated the process for its tender car. The _Salisbury_ was then used to haul out the carts filled with dirt and rock that the convicts were removing from this tunnel.

Using the locomotive to pull the filled carts saved a great deal of time that had been consumed in manually hauling out the removed material. Now, the convicts had more time to dig and shovel the 15-foot-tall tunnel deeper into the mountain.

Meeting in the Middle of a Mountain

The 1800-foot length of the Swannanoa Tunnel was so great that it required two different work crews. One convict crew worked from the western side and another crew worked from the eastern side ... both headed toward the middle. As the convicts dug deeper into the mountain, they could hear the sound deep underground in front of them of the heavy sledge hammers banging on the rock. Each group wanted to be the first to break through to the other. The excitement built as the hammering grew louder and they knew they were getting closer!

The two crews met deep in the heart of Swannanoa Mountain on March 11, 1879. The two long, deep, damp caves had become one very long tunnel. On that same day, Major Wilson sent a telegram to U.S. Senator Zebulon Baird Vance, a mountain native who as Governor of North Carolina a few years earlier had supported the railroad project. The telegram read:

"Daylight entered Buncombe County today through the Swannanoa Tunnel, Grade and centers meet exactly."

The skill and strength necessary for two work crews to start on opposite sides of the mountain digging 15-foot-tall dark caves ... and to meet exactly, deep underground in the middle to form a tunnel one-third mile long ... is both miraculous and amazing!

N.C. Historical Marker for the Swannanoa Tunnel. 2010.

Memorial Marker for Major James W. Wilson
(Now located beside Old Fort Depot). 1972.

The Tough Life of a Prison Inmate Railroad Worker

November 1, 1877 was one of the very few dates when a precise head-count of convicts working on the project was officially recorded. 558 convicts were at work that day in various sites on the Mountain Division: 35 white men, 22 black women, and 501 black men. That ratio was generally maintained.

The convicts were not paid for their work, but in a report to the N.C. Legislature, the construction managers reported that the value of their labor was 98 cents per convict per day. The state could not have afforded to hire workers even at that low wage.

The cost of feeding and supervising the convicts was calculated in a report prepared in December 1878 for a study commission appointed by the North Carolina Legislature. Major Wilson reported that the "actual cost of supporting the convicts up here [on the Mountain Division] is a little under 30 cents per day: feeding, 7 cents; guarding, 10 cents; and the remainder for clothing, medical attention, etc."

An overseer of Lick Log stockade, in a report dated February 1879, stated that an "average day's ration" of food for the convicts was "one-half pound bacon, twenty-two ounces meal, [and either] one-third pound peas or one pound potatoes." A type of coffee drink for the convicts was made of one part ground-up coffee to four parts ground-up rye seeds and thickened with "a considerable quantity of molasses."

Convicts used a lot of tools that had to be purchased with limited money, such as shovels, picks, heavy hammers, rakes, and wooden carts. But the main tools the convicts used were free: flat rocks! Convicts would hold flat rocks and use them to dig and scrape away as much dirt as possible as they flattened out and smoothed the pathway for the cross-ties and rails.

The convicts had very long work days, leaving their stockades "as early as a man can be distinguished," and returning after sunset. Reports from supervisors in 1879 revealed that the work was so hard that convicts were sometimes "willing to undergo punishment to avoid work."

Detailed records of the injuries and deaths of the convicts were not kept, only partly because paper and pencils were not easily obtained. Significantly, the culture of the time did not assign a great value to the life of a convict. With solid rock being blasted, heavy hammers flailing into rock in dark, damp caves and tunnels, and extreme winter temperatures, deaths were inevitable. No doubt there are many unmarked graves out in the woods in places known only to God.

- Open cut east of the Swannanoa Tunnel. 2010.

Breaking Rocks with Fire and Cold Water

Whenever the convicts ran into solid rock while excavating the route for the tracks, they were forced to use spikes and heavy hammers to crack up and clear away the rock. When the area they were working on was not tall enough to require a tunnel, the convicts used a clever way to break up the solid rock masses. They built large fires of soft wood (such as pine, which burns faster than hard woods such as oak and maple) on the solid rock to get it hot.

While some convicts were building soft-wood fires, others were forming a line and passing wooden buckets (also made by the convicts) filled with cold water from streams in the area. This water was poured into large wooden barrels (also made by the convicts) sitting on the top of the rock close to the fires.

When the fire was roaring, convicts would dump the barrels of really cold water onto the hot rock. The cold water dousing the hot fire caused the rock to crack. The convicts then broke up more of the rock with heavy hammers. Sometimes they had to repeat this laborious process.

The open cuts through mostly solid rock would have straight walls on each side of the tracks. When there was more dirt than rock, the sides were sloped.

Some other open cuts were mainly dirt. One of them not far from Round Knob, referred to as Mud Cut, was an especially tall area that was very hard to stabilize. While only partly dug, the sloping wall collapsed after a rain and had to be dug out again. More rain fell, and the dirt wall collapsed again.

This frustrating process repeated several times over a period of many weeks, causing Major Wilson to consider making changes to the route. It became one of the most difficult challenges of the Mountain Division before tons and tons of dirt were dug out and pushed (mainly by hand with flat rocks) downhill out of the way of the tracks.

- Open cut near Round Knob. 1972.

– Tracks through a curved open cut near High Fill. 2010.

Historic and Creative Use of Nobel's Amazing Blasting Oil

Black powder was used to blast away some of the rock in the mountain caves that were being turned into tunnels. However, black powder was too expensive and money was too scarce for it to be used to blast away all the rock masses, even when used sparingly in the tunnels.

Major Wilson had learned of an amazing new product that had been developed by a man from Europe that was even better for blasting rock. Also, it was not as expensive as black powder, probably because most people had not heard of it yet. This new product was called Nobel's Blasting Oil, and Major Wilson bought it to blast solid rock in the tunnels. Today, we refer to Nobel's Blasting Oil by another name: nitroglycerine!

The "blasting oil" was extremely dangerous and had to be handled very carefully. To make it a little safer and easier to handle, Major Wilson instructed the convicts to mix it with some sawdust and a little bit of corn meal ... making a nitroglycerine mash. The mash was somewhat like very thick oatmeal.

To apply the mash for blasting, the convicts carefully poured it into narrow, cylindrical holes about two feet deep that they had previously pounded into the rock with hammer and spike. A wide strip of ground leading to the mash was then cleared and a fuse of dried leaves was laid in the cleared area. The convicts would light the "fuse" and then run like crazy to take cover! The first use of nitroglycerine in the southeastern United States was in the tunnels of the Mountain Division of the Western North Carolina Railroad.

Approximately 18,000 pounds of nitroglycerine mash were produced by the convicts in a shed near Henry Station and carefully taken up the mountain to the tunnels where the blasting was needed. (Alfred Nobel of Sweden, who developed and sold nitroglycerine and dynamite as powerful explosives, later deeply regretted the violent and destructive uses of these products. He used his own money to establish the Nobel Peace Prize to promote peace worldwide.)

Curves and Almost Circles

Determining the curvy route and sloping grade for the rail tracks of the Mountain Division was a huge challenge. In order to keep the grade of the rail bed smooth and level enough to be used by trains, the surveyed route had to be very winding and curvy. After all, the elevation of the track climbs a total of 1,002 feet as it rises from Henry Station and reaches the top of the Eastern Continental Divide at the Swannanoa Tunnel at Ridgecrest.

In order to make this climb useable by trains, the Mountain Division was constructed with a total track curvature of 2,776.4 degrees, the equivalent of almost eight complete circles. The track distance is over 9 miles, even though the straight-line distance from Henry Station to the western portal of the Swannanoa Tunnel is only 3.4 miles.

The most curves in the Mountain Division are found near Round Knob. On the eastern side of Round Knob is a place called High Fill, which is where the largest loop begins and ends. At High Fill, a bird's eye view shows that at the beginning and end of the loop the tracks are only 140 feet apart. From the ground, the upper tracks at High Fill are 120 feet above the tracks at the lower end of the loop. This is the spot where the tracks come the closest to each other after they make a huge loop.

wwwt

High Fill, near Round Knob. 2010. Upper tracks are 140 feet higher
than the lower ones. The tracks are 120 feet apart.

The track winds so much in the Round Knob area that a man-made fountain built in 1885 (and its more famous replacement built in 1910) can be seen in seven different places on different sides of the track! Most of the curves and loops are located in the middle of the Mountain Division. All of the tunnels are in the western 2.5 miles.

The Fountain at Round Knob

In 1885, after the Mountain Division was finished and railroad tracks were laid further toward the North Carolina - Tennessee border, Round Knob Lodge was enlarged and rebuilt as a 5-story hotel! It soon became known all over the country as a fine and grand place to stay. In the summer, it was a cool mountain retreat and in the winter it was a popular destination as a hunters' lodge.

To help people remember Round Knob Lodge, the owners decided to create a large and stunningly attractive fountain beside the hotel and railroad tracks. While riding on the train as it makes its winding curves back and forth between Henry Station and Ridgecrest, the fountain at Round Knob Lodge was visible first on one side of the train and then on the other!

Round Knob Lodge and the fountain, painted 1991 by the late Howard McCurry of Marion, N.C. from a photograph.

The owners of Round Knob Lodge knew they had to compete with some larger and more elaborate hotels in Asheville, North Carolina for customers. Since people going to Asheville by train (the only practical way to get there in the late 1800s) would see the fountain and the 5-story hotel on their way, perhaps they would choose to stay there instead of traveling on to Asheville. Sadly, Round Knob Lodge was destroyed by fire in 1903.

Several years later, George Fisher Baker, a wealthy banker from New York, saw the remains of the burned lodge and non-working fountain as he rode by in the train. Mr. Baker was a friend of Col. Alexander Boyd Andrews, a distinguished and experienced railroad manager from North Carolina. Col. Andrews was quite wealthy, and he had put his personal fortune at risk by guaranteeing payment to assure the construction of the Western North Carolina Railroad between Asheville and Tennessee, west of the Mountain Division.

Mr. Baker decided to use his own money to restore the fountain. When it was finished, he named it after his friend, Col. Andrews. Interestingly, Col. Andrews was involved only in the Western North Carolina Railroad west of Asheville. He was not involved in the construction of the Mountain Division.

The generous Mr. Baker started buying property for the restored fountain in 1910. He acquired a 5-acre tract beside the spot where the fabulous Round Knob Lodge and its well-known fountain had been located. He also bought several more acres about a half-mile up the mountain, plus an easement to connect the two. A small dam was built across a stream on the uphill tract to make a pond.

Underground pipes were laid from the pond down to the site for the re-built fountain so as to create sufficient water pressure for the water to shoot up into the air at the bottom. A pool around the fountain with a unique five-lobed design was constructed in a spot that still would be visible to passengers on the train.

No pumps are used in the man-made geyser. Water pressure from the pond further up the mountain causes the geyser to shoot water to the sky.

The Fountain Becomes Andrews Geyser

In 1911, the new fountain was finished. At a dedication ceremony, it was announced that Mr. Baker was naming this re-built fountain Andrews Geyser, in honor of Col. Andrews, who was present at the ceremony. Dignitaries from the railroad company and from the State of North Carolina were present, along with hundreds of local citizens. Mr. Baker presented the railroad with a deed to the property as a part of the ceremony. The deed contained an important condition that the railroad company must maintain the property in honor of Col. Andrews.

Andrews Geyser continued to delight and amaze railroad passengers for about 60 years until passenger rail service was eventually discontinued around 1971. In 1972, someone closed the valve at the pond that was the source of water for the geyser. When the plume of water was no longer shooting up in the geyser, the railroad stopped maintaining it.

Within a year, mud covered the bottom of the geyser's basin. Soon thereafter, weeds and small bushes began to grow where water used to be. The area around Andrews Geyser grew up with thick bushes and small trees. By 1974, a person could drive by on adjoining Mill Creek Road and never know that Andrews Geyser was only about 50 feet away.

- The scene was shocking after the water stopped flowing, exposing accumulated dirt and mud in the geyser basin. December 1972.

- Weeds and bushes began to grow in the geyser basin in the spring of 1972.

Historical deed research at the McDowell County Courthouse in Marion, NC was done in 1975 by the author, who located a copy of the railroad company's deed for the geyser property. In the deed was the language requiring the company to maintain the geyser as a tribute to Col. Andrews.

The author wrote to Edward T. Breathitt, Jr., former governor of Kentucky who in 1975 was a vice president of Norfolk Southern Railway, and reminded him of the railroad's duty. Instead of resuming maintenance of the geyser property, the railroad chose to give it to the Town of Old Fort as a park. Within weeks, the deed was delivered to Old Fort's mayor in a small ceremony at Town Hall. The Town of Old Fort was proud to become the owner of Andrews Geyser!

The people of Old Fort went to work and cleaned up the area, restoring Andrews Geyser to its former beauty and majesty. It was re-dedicated in a huge ceremony as a bicentennial event on May 16, 1976, with Col. Andrews' grandson in attendance. It now is maintained in memory of Col. Andrews, as Mr. Baker intended when he rebuilt it in 1910 - 1911.

- Volunteers and Old Fort employees worked hard to clean up the area in advance of the re-dedication of Andrews Geyser in May 1976.

Today, Andrews Geyser is a very popular and attractive site for picnics. People begin to get excited when they hear a train whistle in the distance. As the train gets closer, it appears first on one side of the Andrews Geyser park and then on the other. If the train is long, the train cars are visible on both sides of the park at the same time!

To drive to Andrews Geyser, take Exit 73 (Old Fort) from Interstate 40 in McDowell County, NC. (Approximately 30 miles east of Asheville, NC) Go north on Catawba Avenue for one-half mile, into downtown Old Fort. Turn left after crossing the railroad tracks (the restored Old Fort Depot is on the left, beside the giant arrowhead) and go west on U.S. Highway 70 for 3/10 mile. Turn right onto Old US Highway 70 and go west for 2.4 miles. Turn right onto Mill Creek Road (the site of Henry Station is in the field on the right) and travel 2.1 miles. The park is on the left. There is a large grassy area around the concrete basin of the geyser with many picnics tables in the shelter of surrounding shade trees. There is no admission charge to enjoy having a picnic at Andrews Geyser, but there are no restrooms or concessions.

- N.C. Historical Marker for Andrews Geyser. 1976.

– Andrews Geyser in July 2010.

Wrapping it Up

Andy's Grandpa was really proud that Major Wilson had both the skill and the determination to design and lead the construction of the Mountain Division. He didn't mind at all that he was proven wrong when he told Andy the railroad couldn't be built up the Eastern Continental Divide.

The construction of the Mountain Division of the Western North Carolina Railroad accomplished what seemed to be impossible. Using measuring systems and instruments that today are crude, and using hard physical labor and only the most basic tools, this huge project was undertaken and successfully completed. The hard work was intense and the conditions were severe, but the railroad that couldn't be built was built.

The dedicated work and determination at a time when the State of North Carolina and the United States of America both were struggling to become united after the blistering civil war was one of the finest achievements in the history of our region, our state and our country.

Primary Historical References

Tunnels, Nitro and Convicts is based on condensed historical information and research from the author, primarily in 1972 while a history major at Wake Forest University, including:

(1) The Mountain Division of the Western North Carolina Railroad: Experiment in Hardship, written 1972 and copyrighted 1976 by Stephen R. (Steve) Little. Quoted material in the text comes from this manuscript.

(2) Andrews Geyser: Symbol of New Life, written and copyrighted 1976 by Stephen R. (Steve) Little.

Photo Credits:

Photograph of Henry Station was provided courtesy of Peggy Silvers of Old Fort, North Carolina.

Photograph of the crew of local men outside Burgin Tunnel, was provided courtesy of Becky Garrou of McDowell County, North Carolina, great granddaughter of the man on the left.

The following two photographs were taken by Rufus Morgan and are from the North Carolina Collection, University of North Carolina Library in Chapel Hill, North Carolina and are included with the UNC Library's permission: Lick Log Tunnel, and the _Salisbury_ pulling passengers and frieght near Old Fort

All other photographs dated between 1971 and 2010 were taken by the author.

Acknowledgments:

The author gratefully acknowledges and expresses appreciation for the support and suggestions of:

Alice Hobbs Little, wife of the author
Sally Little and Mary Little, daughters of the author
John Brown, friend of the author from Ridgecrest, NC
Cate Powell Sawyer, niece of the author from Raleigh, NC
Steve Pierce, friend of the author from Marion, NC
Larry Mock, friend of the author from Marion, NC

Printed in the United States
by Baker & Taylor Publisher Services